Amazing Habitats

POLAR LANDS

Franklin Watts
Published in Great Britain in 2017
by The Watts Publishing Group

Copyright © 2014
Brown Bear Books Ltd

Author: Leon Gray
Designer: Karen Perry
Picture Researcher: Clare Newman
Editor: Tim Harris
Children's Publisher: Anne O'Daly
Design Manager: Keith Davis
Editorial Director: Lindsey Lowe

ISBN: 978-1-4451-3693-6

Dewey no. 577'.0911

Printed in China

Franklin Watts
An imprint of
Hachette Children's Group
Part of The Watts Publishing Group
Carmelite House
50 Victoria Embankment
London EC4Y 0DZ

An Hachette UK Company
www.hachette.co.uk
www.franklinwatts.co.uk

Note to parents and teachers concerning
websites: In the book every effort has been
made by the Publishers to ensure that
websites are suitable for children, that they
are of the highest educational value, and that
they contain no inappropriate or offensive
material. However, because of the nature of
the Internet, it is impossible to guarantee that
the contents of these sites will not be altered.
We advise that Internet access is supervised
by a responsible adult.

CONTENTS

INTRODUCTION

The world's polar regions are the frozen seas and lands of the Arctic near the North Pole and the icy continent of Antarctica near the South Pole.

ICE BIRDS

Adelie penguins live on sea ice in the Southern Ocean and around the coast of Antarctica. These birds spend most of their lives in the icy water, hunting shrimp-like animals called **krill**.

The places where animals and plants live and grow are called **habitats**. Some animals and plants live in rivers and lakes or tropical rainforests. Some live in polar lands. Polar lands are some of the coldest places on our planet. In fact, the land around the North and South Poles is so cold that it is permanently frozen. In the Arctic **tundra**, further away from the North Pole, the temperature is milder during the summer, when the ice melts.

Read on to find out what the polar lands are like – and how plants, animals and people live in them.

A lot of ice thaws during the Arctic summer to reveal a wet, swampy landscape.

WORLD POLAR

This map shows the world's polar regions bounded by the Arctic Circle in the north and the Antarctic Circle in the south.

NORTH POLE

ARCTIC CIRCLE

NORTH AMERICA

SOUTH AMERICA

ANTARCTIC CIRCLE

SOUTH POLE

Polar bears are top **predators** that live on Arctic land and sea ice in areas such as Hudson Bay, Canada.

During the summer, much of the sea ice melts to reveal the rocky coastline of Antarctica.

Brown Station is a scientific research centre in Paradise Bay, Antarctica.

LANDS

People from the town of Tasiilaq in Greenland have adapted to the harsh Arctic climate.

Polar lands

ARCTIC OCEAN

EUROPE

ASIA

AFRICA

The island of Spitsbergen is a breeding ground for many Arctic seabirds.

AUSTRALIA

Emperor penguins raise their chicks in colonies on mainland Antarctica.

SOUTHERN OCEAN

ANTARCTICA

CLIMATE

The climate in the Arctic and Antarctica is bitterly cold, even during the summer. Since hardly any rain or snow falls in these places, they are called polar **deserts**.

The Arctic and Antarctica are so cold because the North and South poles receive little direct light from the Sun. In each pole's summer season, the Sun does not dip below the **horizon**. It shines for 24 hours a day, but the Sun is so low in the sky that it cannot warm up the area around the poles. In addition, the thick layer of ice and snow reflects much of the sunlight back into space. In each pole's winter season, the Sun is hidden below the horizon. The temperature plunges as the polar region becomes dark.

BRAVE BIRD
Emperor penguins nest in colonies inland from the Antarctic coast in winter. In summer, they return to the ocean.

In the polar regions, the air is so cold that it freezes the water in your breath.

WOW!

• The coldest temperature ever recorded on Earth was in Antarctica: −89.2°C (−129°F) at Vostok in 1983.

• Sometimes, winds blow from the Antarctic mountains towards the sea at 300 km/h (190 mph). That is faster than the wind in a hurricane.

Polar deserts

Even though they are classed as deserts, there is a lot of water in both polar regions. Most of this water stays frozen on the surface of the land as ice and snow. Since the polar regions are so cold, water cannot **evaporate** from the icy surface. Because the air is so dry, it rarely rains or snows. Antarctica is one of the driest places on the planet. At the South Pole, less than 5 cm (2 in) of rain and snow falls each year.

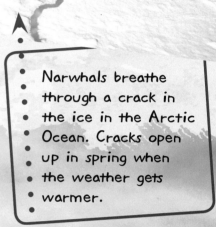

Narwhals breathe through a crack in the ice in the Arctic Ocean. Cracks open up in spring when the weather gets warmer.

Breaking ice

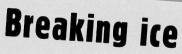

Chunks of ice up to 60 metres (200 feet) high break off the ice sheets around Antarctica and Greenland in the Arctic. This is called calving. If Earth's temperature gets warmer, bigger chunks will break off and float away.

DRY LAND
Some areas of Antarctica are so dry that they are free of ice. The McMurdo Dry Valleys are the driest places of all in Antarctica.

11

PLANTS

Only the toughest plants can survive in polar lands. They have **adapted** to the cold, dark polar winter and life with little rainfall.

COTTON SEED

A field of cotton grass is a common sight in the Arctic summer. It survives in winter because snow covers it and **insulates** it from the coldest temperatures.

Plants need light and water to survive. They use the energy from sunlight to make food from water and carbon dioxide gas. This process is called **photosynthesis**. In the polar regions, it is dark for most of the winter. The plants that do live in polar regions have adapted to these extremes. In the Arctic, most plants complete their short **life cycles** in the summer. They die or remain inactive in the harsh winter and grow back the following summer.

A polar bear roams through a field of fireweed in the Arctic tundra.

Fruity food

Crowberries are an important source of food for bears and other animals that live in the Arctic tundra. The tough, black berries start to appear in July and continue to grow until the first winter snow falls in October.

Pearlwort is one of only two flowering plants that grow in Antarctica.

Antarctic plants

The Arctic summer provides a short growing season for some hardy plants. Life in Antarctica is much more extreme. Even so, plant-like **organisms** called **algae** can survive. Algae do not have roots, stems or leaves. Instead, they grow on the surface of rocks. Mosses also cling to rocks. During the short summer, these plants cover rocks along the shore. In turn, the moss carpets provide habitats for the two flowering plants that live in Antarctica – pearlwort and Antarctic hairgrass.

BIO FACT
Trees cannot grow in polar regions. The cold is too extreme and their large roots cannot push through the frozen soil.

Mountain habitats

In many ways, life on high mountains, such as the Alps in Europe, is similar to the extremes of the Arctic tundra. Snow covers the high peaks, the temperature is bitterly cold and fierce winds batter the slopes. Many plants that can survive the Arctic tundra, such as purple saxifrage (below), also grow high up on alpine mountains.

Colourful purple saxifrage flowers bloom during the Arctic summer.

ANIMALS

Few animals can survive the extreme polar climate. The biggest challenge is keeping warm – only the hardiest animals stay all year round. Most move away in the harsh winter.

During the summer, the soil in Antarctica is permanently frozen. No plants can grow on the land, so there is little food to support animal life. In fact, the only animals that can survive on the Antarctic mainland all year round are tiny insects and **mites**.

In the Arctic, the summer is slightly warmer and for two short months the icy topsoil melts in some places. Then, the tundra bursts into life with plants, insects, birds, and **mammals** such as reindeer and bears. In autumn, the tundra freezes solid again and many Arctic animals **migrate** south to escape the harsh winter.

Lemmings are one of the few mammals that can survive the harsh Arctic winter. They stay warm by living in burrows.

FUR COATS

Reindeer that live in the Arctic tundra are covered with two layers of fur to protect them from the cold – a dense undercoat and a less dense top layer of longer hairs.

On the move

Birds have an advantage over many other animals because they can fly very long distances. Many species migrate to the Arctic tundra during the mild summer and fly south before winter sets in. The spoon-billed sandpiper (left) is a rare bird that breeds in Siberia, Russia, during the summer months. As winter approaches, the birds fly south to Bangladesh.

Arctic predators

Animals such as foxes, wolves (above), polar bears and owls are top of the Arctic **food chain**. The Arctic fox hunts a wide range of animals, including lemmings, fish, seals and seabirds. Arctic foxes also eat berries and other plants when animal food is scarce. The polar bear is the most formidable Arctic predator. These mammals spend much of their time in the cold Arctic Ocean, hunting their favourite food – seals.

COAT COLOUR

The Arctic wolf has a thick layer of fur to keep it warm. Its white fur is thicker in the winter months when the weather is at its coldest. White fur helps to **camouflage** the wolf in the snow.

The white bear

Polar bears are top predators of the Arctic tundra. These huge mammals grow up to 2 metres (7ft) tall and weigh more than 500 kg (1,110lb). Polar bears have a thick layer of **blubber** under their skin to keep them warm. They also have dense fur to trap heat around their bodies.

Thick fur coat

Good vision

Sensitve nose

Sharp claws

19

Antarctic animals

Most Antarctic animals live near the coast and rely on food from the ocean to survive. Seals prey on fish near the Antarctic coastline and come ashore to rest. Adelie and emperor penguins are also found in the ocean, where they hunt fish, but venture onto the land to roost and **brood**. Unhatched and baby penguins are then vulnerable to seabirds, such as petrels and skuas, which eat penguin eggs and chicks.

FOOD CHAIN

Seals are a vital link in the Antarctic food chain. Seals eat animals such as fish, squid and krill. In turn, seals are food for predators, such as killer whales.

South polar skuas are deadly predators. They feed on penguin chicks, other seabirds and even the chicks of other skuas!

Good eyesight

Sharp beak

Short, broad tail

Partially webbed feet

Doting dad!

During the bitter Antarctic winter. male emperor penguins clamber onto the mainland to brood their eggs. while the females return to the sea to feed.

PEOPLE

The only people who live in Antarctica are in research stations because the climate is so severe. But some people have adapted to life in the Arctic tundra.

People have lived in the Arctic for thousands of years. Different groups live in different places. For example, the Chukchi and Nenet live in the Siberian Arctic. The Yupik live around the Bering Sea, between Siberia and Alaska. Since there are so few plants, Arctic people rely on animals for food and clothing to keep warm. Their way of life has changed dramatically as other people have arrived. They inhabit both a traditional and a modern world.

Inuit hunters

The Inuit are a group of people who live in the eastern parts of the Canadian Arctic. In the past, Inuit hunters used harpoons and bows and arrows to kill sea mammals, such as seals. Today, they use guns.

In summer, Inuit people dry fish on racks to preserve it for the winter.

DOG SLED

In the past, people living in the Arctic used dog sleds to get around. Today, they are more likely to travel on a snowmobile.

Polar science

Many countries have set up research bases in polar regions to explore this mysterious land. Some researchers are studying the harsh climate to learn how Antarctic animals can survive in extreme places. Others are exploring ways to exploit the reserves of **crude oil** that may be buried beneath the frozen ground.

Modern world

Life has changed for people living in the Arctic. Motorised transport such as snowmobiles and petrol-powered boats have replaced many of the dog sleds and wooden fishing vessels. In fact, many people have stopped hunting and buy their food in shops. Even the **igloo** – a shelter carved from blocks of ice – has been replaced with modern timber-framed houses.

BIO FACT
When European explorers arrived in the Arctic, they brought illnesses such as **tuberculosis**. Many Arctic people died because they caught these deadly diseases.

A traditional wooden fishing boat leaves the harbour at Reine in the Norwegian Lofoten islands.

THE FUTURE

The polar regions are some of our planet's most unspoiled natural wilderness areas. But human activities are destroying these precious habitats and the wildlife that lives in them.

One of the biggest threats to polar habitats is **global warming**. As more people burn more **fossil fuels** to power factories and motor cars, our planet's temperature is slowly increasing. Many scientists think this is melting the ice around the Arctic and Antarctica. Animals, such as penguins and polar bears, may struggle to survive in a changed environment. As the melting ice flows into the ocean, the water level is rising. Many low-lying islands and coastal habitats may flood, and people may lose their homes.

BEAUTY SPOT

Alaska is an area of outstanding beauty, but mining and other activities threaten to harm these important natural habitats.

Oil rigs, such as this one in Prudhoe Bay, Alaska, USA, are becoming a common sight in the Arctic.

QUIZ

Try this quiz to test your knowledge of polar lands. Find the answers on page 31.

1 Can you name two parts of a polar bear's body that keep it warm in the freezing Arctic climate?

2 In polar regions, your face becomes covered with ice if you spend too long outside. Why is this?

3 What is the name of this predatory seabird that lives on the Antarctic coast?

4 What is the name of this plant that produces colourful purple flowers?

Fact File

- The world's polar lands are the Arctic in the north and Antarctica in the south.
- The Antarctic is also called a desert because hardly any rain falls.
- Since the Arctic tundra is milder than the climate in Antarctica, more animals and plants can survive there.

Winners and losers

⬆ Birds are some of the most successful polar animals. They migrate to warmer places during the harsh winter.

⬇ Polar bears and penguins could soon die out because of global warming. Earth's rising temperature is melting the sea ice on which these animals depend.

5 What weapons did Arctic people use to hunt with before they had guns?

29

GLOSSARY

adapted: When an organism slowly changes to fit in with its surroundings.

algae: Tiny plant-like organisms that live in polar regions. Algae are food for the animals that live there.

blubber: Layer of fat between the skin and muscle.

brood: The way birds sit on eggs to keep them warm until they hatch.

camouflage: The way some animals blend in with their surroundings.

crude oil: A dark oil dug up from beneath Earth's surface and used as a fuel for motor cars and machines.

deserts: Places on Earth that have less than 25 cm (10 in) of rainfall every year.

evaporate: To change from a liquid to a gas.

food chain: The order in which animals feed on plants and other animals within a habitat.

fossil fuels: Fuels made from the remains of dead animals and plants that lived millions of years ago.

global warming: Gradual increase in the Earth's temperature caused by human activities, such as burning fossil fuels.

habitats: The places where plants or animals usually live and grow.

horizon: The line at which Earth's surface and the sky appear to meet.

igloo: A dome-shaped house made from blocks of snow and ice.

krill: Tiny shrimp-like ocean animals that are food for other sea creatures.

insulates: Keeps it warmer than it otherwise would be.

life cycles: The series of changes in an organism's life, from birth to death.

mammals: Animals with warm blood that breathe air using lungs. Mammals feed their young on milk.

migrate: To move from one place to another according to the seasons.

mites: Tiny bugs with eight legs.

organisms: A scientific word to describe any living thing.

photosynthesis: The process by which plants make food using the energy from sunlight.

predator: Animal that hunts and eats other animals.

tuberculosis: A deadly disease that affects the lungs.

tundra: A vast area in the Arctic where there are no trees but small plants can grow close to the ground.

FURTHER RESOURCES

Books

Guillain. Charlotte. *Polar Regions (Explorer Travel Guides)*. Raintree (2014).

Johnson. Jinny. *Watery Worlds: Polar Seas*. Franklin Watts (2012).

Newland. Sonya. *Saving Wildlife: Polar Animals*. Franklin Watts (2014).

Woolf. Alex. *Travelling Wild: Expedition to the Arctic*. Wayland (2014).

Websites

BBC Nature. This website is a great source of information about the planet's northern and southern extremes. Click on the links to see stunning photos and videos of some of the animals and plants that live in these inhospitable habitats.
www.bbc.co.uk/nature/habitats/Polar_region

Discovering Antarctica. Find out all about this undiscovered continent and what we can do to protect it for the future. Includes interactive quizzes to test your knowledge.
www.discoveringantarctica.org.uk

National Geographic. Find out where polar bears live. what they eat. how they survive the in freezing temperatures. Includes links to related National Geographic pages.
http://www.ngkids.co.uk/animals/polar-bear-facts

WorldWide Fund for Nature. Photos. videos. animals and plants that live in the world's polar regions. Read about some of the conservation plans for the Arctic and Antarctica, and find out what you can do to help.
http://www.worldwildlife.org/habitats/polar-regions

Answers to the Quiz: **1** Blubber and fur. **2** The water in your breath freezes. **3** South polar skua. **4** Purple saxifrage. **5** Harpoons and bows and arrows.

INDEX